CONNECT BIBLE STUDIES

TV Game Shows

Who Wants to be a Millionaire?
Survivor
The Weakest Link
Big Brother

www.connectbiblestudies.com

connect

linking the Word to the world

CONNECT BIBLE STUDIES: TV Game Shows

Published in this format by Scripture Union, 207-209 Queensway, Bletchley, MK2 2EB, England.

Scripture Union is an international Christian charity working with churches in more than 130 countries providing resources to bring the good news about Jesus Christ to children, young people and families — and to encourage them to develop spiritually through the Bible and prayer.

As well as a network of volunteers, staff and associates who run holidays, church-based events and school Christian groups, Scripture Union produces a wide range of publications and supports those who use the resources through training programmes.

Email: info@scriptureunion.org.uk
Internet: www.scriptureunion.org.uk

© Damaris Trust, PO Box 200, Southampton, SO17 2DL.

Damaris Trust enables people to relate Christian faith and contemporary culture. It helps them to think about the issues within society from a Christian perspective and to explore God's truth as it is revealed in the Bible. Damaris provides resources via the Internet, workshops, publications and products.

Email: office@damaris.org
Internet: www.damaris.org

ALSO AVAILABLE AS AN ELECTRONIC DOWNLOAD: www.connectbiblestudies.com

Chief editor: Nick Pollard
Consultant Editor: Andrew Clark
Managing Editor: Di Archer
Written by Di Archer, Caroline Puntis, Tony Watkins

First published 2001
ISBN 1 85999 609 4

British Library Cataloguing-in-Publication Data: a catalogue record for this book is available from the British Library.

Cover design and print production by:
CPO, Garcia Estate, Canterbury Road, Worthing, West Sussex BN13 1BW.

Other titles in this series:

Harry Potter and the Goblet of Fire ISBN 1 85999 578 0
The Matrix ISBN 1 85999 579 9
U2: All that you can't leave behind ISBN 1 85999 580 2
Billy Elliot ISBN 1 85999 581 0
Chocolat ISBN 1 85999 608 6
How to be Good ISBN 1 85999 610 8
Destiny's Child: Survivor ISBN 1 85999 613 2

And more titles following — check www.connectbiblestudies.com for latest titles or ask at any good Christian bookshop.

connect

linking the Word to the world

Using Connect Bible Studies

What Are These Studies?

These innovative home group Bible studies have two aims. Firstly, we design them to enable group members to dig into their Bibles and get to know them better. Secondly, we aim to help members to think through topical issues in a Biblical way. Hence the studies are based on a current popular book or film etc. The issues raised by these are the subjects for the Bible studies.

We do not envisage that all members will always be able to watch the films or read the books, or indeed that they will always want to. A summary is always provided. However, our vision is that knowing about these films and books empowers Christians to engage with friends and colleagues about them. Addressing issues from a Biblical perspective gives Christians confidence that they know what they think, and can bring a distinctive angle to bear in conversations.

The studies are produced in sets of four—*ie* four weeks' worth of group Bible Study material. These are available in print published by Scripture Union from your local Christian bookshop, or via the Internet at www.connectbiblestudies.com. Anyone can sign up for a free monthly email newsletter that announces the new studies and provides other information (sign up on the Connect Bible Studies website at www.connectbiblestudies.com/uk/register).

How Do I Use Them?

We design the studies to stimulate creative thought and discussion within a Biblical context. Each section therefore has a range of questions or options from which you as leader may choose in order to tailor the study to your group's needs and desires. Different approaches may appeal at different times, so the studies aim to supply lots of choice. Whilst adhering to the main aim of corporate Bible study, some types of questions may enable this for your group better than others—so take your pick.

Group members should be supplied with the appropriate sheet that they can fill in, each one also showing the relevant summary.

Leader's notes contain:

1. Opening Questions

These help your group settle in to discussion, whilst introducing the topics. They may be straightforward, personal or creative, but are aiming to provoke a response.

2. Summary

We suggest the summary of the book or film will follow now, read aloud if necessary. There may well be reactions that group members want to express even before getting on to the week's issue.

3. Key Issue

Again, either read from the leader's notes, or summarised.

4. Bible Study

Lots of choice here. Choose as appropriate to suit your group — get digging into the Bible. Background reading and texts for further help and study are suggested, but please use the material provided to inspire your group to explore their Bibles as much as possible. A concordance might be a handy standby for looking things up. A commentary could be useful too, such as the New Bible Commentary 21st century edition (IVP, 1994). The idea is to help people to engage with the truth of God's word, wrestling with it if necessary but making it their own.

Don't plan to work through every question here. Within each section the two questions explore roughly the same ground but from different angles or in different ways. Our advice is to take one question from each section. The questions are open–ended so each ought to yield good discussion—though of course any discussion in a Bible study may need prompting to go a little further.

5. Implications

Here the aim is to tie together the perspectives gained through Bible study and the impact of the book or film. The implications may be personal, a change in worldview, or new ideas for relating to non–churchgoers. Choose questions that adapt to the flow of the discussion.

6. Prayer

Leave time for it! We suggest a time of open prayer, or praying in pairs if the group would prefer. Encourage your members to focus on issues from your study that had a particular impact on them. Try different approaches to prayer—light a candle, say a prayer each, write prayers down, play quiet worship music—aim to facilitate everyone to relate to God.

7. Background Reading

You will find links to some background reading on the Connect Bible Studies website: www.connectbiblestudies.com/

8. Online Discussion

You can discuss the studies online with others on the Connect Bible Studies website at www.connectbiblestudies.com/discuss/

www.connectbiblestudies.com

linking the Word to the world

TV Game Shows

Part One: Who Wants To Be A Millionaire?

Why shouldn't you have a windfall in your life? We're not saying, 'This is the alternative to work'. But an awful lot of people's lives are dreadfully dreary and I think if you can put a bit of extra fun and pleasure into it, why the hell not?
(Chris Tarrant, Observer, 02/04/00)

Please read Using Connect Bible Studies *before leading a Bible study using this material.*

Opening Questions

Choose one of these questions.

What would you do with a million pounds?	Name three things you consider to be luxury items.
How often do you watch the show? Why?	Would you like to have a go on the show? How do you think you would do?

Summary

'Is that your final answer?' probes quiz host Chris Tarrant, often causing the contestant to lapse into renewed doubt — should they risk losing some of their winnings or take the money and run? Much of *Who Wants to be a Millionaire*'s success is due to Tarrant's skilful handling of crunch moments, where many thousands of pounds are at stake.

To have an opportunity to win the million pounds, the contestant must first get through the tricky 'fastest finger' round and beat the other nine hopefuls to the button. In order to win the jackpot, fifteen multiple-choice questions have to be answered correctly in a row — the moment a question is answered wrongly the game is over. The first question is worth £100. Thereafter, the stakes are more or less doubled with each question until a million pounds is up for grabs. There are 'guarantee points' along the way at £1000 and £32,000, to which the contestant will fall back if they answer a question incorrectly. However, if they are struggling to choose from the four possible answers help is at hand in the form of three lifelines — 'Phone a Friend', '50:50' and 'Ask the Audience'. When these are used up, the contestant is on their own. They can retire at any stage with their winnings, or keep going in the hope that they will take home the million. Two contestants in the UK have won £1 million since the show began in 1998.

Key Issue: Money

Who Wants to be a Millionaire? Presumably the reply to this question is 'everyone', judging by the popularity of this game show around the world. Potential participants ring a prime rate number and try to answer a general knowledge question that assesses their suitability for the show. Viewers are in their millions too, captivated by the tension and opportunity of the show. Is there anyone who would turn down the chance of an easy million pounds? The producers of the show have obviously hit on a winning formula, so what is the appeal? What is the attraction of big money? Are the winners likely to be satisfied with their gains, or is there more to life? Does the Bible condemn all this as greed, or does it have more to say? Who wants to be a Christian millionaire?

Bible Study

Choose one question from each section. Note that one question in each of the sections relates to the early chapters of Ecclesiastes. You may like to focus on these throughout your study.

1.   Why is Money So Appealing?

*It's not enough to change your life, but it's made it a hell of a lot easier ...
We've paid off our debts, had a couple of holidays, and it's meant that my
husband doesn't have to work every weekend to meet the bills.*
(Fiona Wheeler, contestant, www.itv.co.uk)

- ◆   Read Genesis 3:17–19; Proverbs 14:20; Ecclesiastes 2:4–10. What are the apparent advantages of being wealthy?

- ◆   Read Luke 12:16–19. What kind of life is the rich man hoping to make for himself? How does he feel about what he has achieved?

2.   Giving in to Greed

*I don't have a problem with people winning lots of money. I think it's actually
very good for them.* (Chris Tarrant, *The Observer*, 02/04/00)

- ◆   Read Ecclesiastes 4:4; 5:8–12. What is the nature of greed? How does it affect individuals and communities?

- ◆   Read Luke 12:13–21. What triggered the rich man's greed? What does Jesus say about storing up an abundance of possessions?

3. Winner or Loser?

I honestly thought I knew the answer but obviously I was wrong ... I know £93,000 is a ridiculous sum of money to lose but don't forget I still went home with £32,000 — that's a huge amount of money to me and my wife.
(Jim Titmuss, contestant, www.itv.co.uk)

- ◆ Read Ecclesiastes 5:13–6:12. Does the writer of Ecclesiastes see wealth as a good or a bad thing?

- ◆ Read James 5:1–6. Why are the rich condemned? What is the value of wealth?

    See also Matthew 6:19–21.

4. God's Economy

I arrived with nothing so it didn't matter if I left with nothing.
(Davy Young, contestant, www.itv.co.uk)

- ◆ Read Ecclesiastes 5:13–6:12. What are the keys to dealing with wealth and possessions?

- ◆ Read Matthew 6:19–34. Jesus says we have a fundamental choice to make about what we pursue in life. Where do our choices lead us? What is a healthy attitude to treasure on earth?

Implications

The wonderful thing about winning, for me, is that I feel very much more secure. It is wonderful not having to worry about money.
(Judith Keppel, millionaire, *The Daily Telegraph*, 12/04/01)

Choose one or more of the following questions.

♦   Is it wrong to enter a competition to win money/a free holiday/free goods/etc?

♦   Do you worry about money? How much does it affect your sense of security?

♦   What is luxury? How do you relate to God in the middle of it?

♦   Why do we get greedy? How can we be free from it?

♦   How do we deal with the tension of living in a world where twenty per cent of the population consumes eighty per cent of its resources?

♦   What would you say to friends who claim their troubles would be over if only they could win that million pounds?

Prayer

Spend some time praying through these issues.

Background Reading

You will find links to some background reading on the Connect Bible Studies website: www.connectbiblestudies.com/uk/catalogue/0006/background.htm

Discuss

Discuss this study in the online discussion forums at www.connectbiblestudies.com/discuss

Members' Sheet 1: *Who Wants to be a Millionaire?*

Summary

'Is that your final answer?' probes quiz host Chris Tarrant, often causing the contestant to lapse into renewed doubt — should they risk losing some of their winnings or take the money and run? Much of *Who Wants to be a Millionaire*'s success is due to Tarrant's skilful handling of crunch moments, where many thousands of pounds are at stake.

To have an opportunity to win the million pounds, the contestant must first get through the tricky 'fastest finger' round and beat the other nine hopefuls to the button. In order to win the jackpot, fifteen multiple-choice questions have to be answered correctly in a row — the moment a question is answered wrongly the game is over. The first question is worth £100. Thereafter, the stakes are more or less doubled with each question until a million pounds is up for grabs. There are 'guarantee points' along the way at £1000 and £32,000, to which the contestant will fall back if they answer a question incorrectly. However, if they are struggling to choose from the four possible answers help is at hand in the form of three lifelines — 'Phone a Friend', '50:50' and 'Ask the Audience'. When these are used up, the contestant is on their own. They can retire at any stage with their winnings, or keep going in the hope that they will take home the million. Two contestants in the UK have won £1 million since the show began in 1998.

Key Issue

Bible Study notes

Implications

Prayer

connect

linking the Word to the world

TV Game Shows

Part Two: Survivor

That's the way it goes — it's about surviving.
It's not really about being nice to people.
(James, 40, Helang tribe)

Please read Using Connect Bible Studies *before leading a Bible study using this material.*

Opening Questions

Choose one of these questions.

What luxury item would you have taken to the island?	How well would you survive on a desert island?
Would you rather lead or be led?	Do you watch *Survivor*? Why?

Summary

'Trust no one' is this Reality TV show's pertinent slogan. Stranded for forty days and nights on Pulau Tiga, a remote island in the South China Sea, sixteen 'survivors' have to fend for themselves. With only a forty-day supply of rice and limited equipment for catching the elusive fish, sometimes there is only rat on the menu. But while they depend on each other for survival, the players are also competing to win £1 million. Every three days one of their number is voted off the island. The procedure and rules of the game have been skilfully developed so that no contestant is ever truly free from the threat of eviction.

During the first stages of the game, two 'tribes' of eight people — Helang and Ular — compete directly against each other. Life on the island revolves around a three-day cycle of events — Reward Challenge, Immunity Challenge, Tribal Council. The Reward Challenge is crucial in building morale, especially when the prize is food. Winning immunity on the second day means exemption from Tribal Council on the third. It is then down to the losing tribe to vote one of their own members off the island, leaving them in a weaker position for the next round of challenges. Once six people have been voted off the island the two groups combine into a single tribe — Sekutu. The cycle continues as before, but now the general rule is 'every man for himself'.

The survivors are allowed to discuss their votes freely and make alliances. The result is an intriguing melodrama that makes compulsive viewing — from the comfort of a living-room armchair.

Key Issue: Survival of the Fittest

The *Survivor* programme taps into a whole range of human interactions. It is a game which appears to demand a raft of skills from its competitors. The final survivor must have passed physical, mental and relational tests which are both individual and corporate. The winner must be strong, yet not too strong; clever, yet not too clever — or fellow competitors will vote them out. This survival challenge is a complex one. Does it appeal because sometimes life for us all can feel very mundane? How do we survive hostile, competitive situations? When do we work together, and when do we put ourselves first? Does the end justify the means? What does 'survival' really mean anyway? Is that what God designed us for?

Bible Study

Choose one question from each section.

1. Surviving Together — Teamwork

On Helang beach a new day is dawning. For this tribe, life can only get better. Suddenly they've realised the value of working together — a new spirit they must now develop if they're to have any chance of winning today's Immunity Challenge. (Mark Austin, presenter)

 ♦   Read Nehemiah 2:17–3:2; 4:6–23. What factors contributed to the team's success in rebuilding the wall? What motivated them to overcome difficulties?

 When Babylon became the dominant power in the Near East in 605 BC, they took some of the people of Judah into exile. Later, in 586 BC, they destroyed Jerusalem and deported many more people. After the Babylonian Empire fell to the Persians in 538 BC, King Cyrus issued a decree that the exiles could return to Jerusalem. Ezra went there in 458 BC and under his leadership the people set about rebuilding the temple. A few years later — in 445 BC — Nehemiah also went to Jerusalem and led the people in rebuilding the city walls.

 ♦   Read Ephesians 4:1–16. What reason does Paul give for the diversity of roles within the body? What is the goal of this team?

2. Surviving at all Costs — Competition

When it comes down to it, if it's a million pounds and there's four or five people left on the island I'll be thinking of every wicked trick I can.
(James, 40, Helang tribe)

♦   Read Genesis 25:21–34 and 27:1–38. Why does Jacob go to such lengths to trick Isaac? Does the end justify the means?

♦   Read 1 Corinthians 3:1–23. What spirit of competition did Paul challenge? Why? In what way were the Corinthians deceived?

3. Surviving Others — Deceit

I'm not naturally a very devious person but I am a very, very good liar.
(Eve, 29, Ular tribe)

♦   Read Luke 22:1–6 and Matthew 26:20–25; 47–50; 27:1–10. What loyalties was Judas betraying? What were the consequences of this betrayal for Jesus, himself and the team of disciples?

♦   Read Acts 5:1–11. What was at the heart of Ananias' and Sapphira's deception and why didn't they succeed? How did it affect the rest of the community?

4. The Survival Instinct

I'm here to play a game. I'm here to play it hard and I'm here to play it as well as I possibly can. I'm not interested in a tan, I'm not interested in lying on a beach. I'm here to win. (Andy, 41, Helang tribe)

♦   Read Daniel 3:1–30. How desperate were Shadrach, Meshach and Abednego to survive? Why?

♦   Read Romans 8:28–39. What is Paul's attitude to survival? What determines his priorities?

See also Philippians 1:18b–26.

Implications

If you have got to be a really nasty piece of work to win that million pounds, I'd rather go home poor and happy and a nice person than be a complete *!?@* and win it. (Eve, 30, Ular tribe)

Choose one or more of the following questions.

♦ The temptation to deceive others can be very appealing. Is the 'little white lie' ever justified?

♦ To feel betrayed is such a painful emotion. Are there people you need to forgive? Or confessions you need to make?

♦ How well do you work as part of a team? What needs to change? How can you develop the gifts God has given you for the sake of others?

♦ Is a spirit of competition ever appropriate? How do we deal with, say, colleagues back-stabbing at work, or scheming to get promoted?

♦ Do you trust God for your physical as well as your spiritual well-being?

♦ How would you answer a neighbour who thinks *Survivor* shows that humans are basically competitive and selfish?

Prayer

Spend some time praying through these issues.

Background Reading

You will find links to some background reading on the Connect Bible Studies website: www.connectbiblestudies.com/uk/catalogue/0006/background.htm

Discuss

Discuss this study in the online discussion forums at www.connectbiblestudies.com/discuss

Members' Sheet 2: *Survivor*

Summary

'Trust no one' is this Reality TV show's pertinent slogan. Stranded for forty days and nights on Pulau Tiga, a remote island in the South China Sea, sixteen 'survivors' have to fend for themselves. With only a forty-day supply of rice and limited equipment for catching the elusive fish, sometimes there is only rat on the menu. But while they depend on each other for survival, the players are also competing to win £1 million. Every three days one of their number is voted off the island. The procedure and rules of the game have been skilfully developed so that no contestant is ever truly free from the threat of eviction.

During the first stages of the game, two 'tribes' of eight people — Helang and Ular — compete directly against each other. Life on the island revolves around a three-day cycle of events — Reward Challenge, Immunity Challenge, Tribal Council. The Reward Challenge is crucial in building morale, especially when the prize is food. Winning immunity on the second day means exemption from Tribal Council on the third. It is then down to the losing tribe to vote one of their own members off the island, leaving them in a weaker position for the next round of challenges. Once six people have been voted off the island the two groups combine into a single tribe — Sekutu. The cycle continues as before, but now the general rule is 'every man for himself'.

The survivors are allowed to discuss their votes freely and make alliances. The result is an intriguing melodrama that makes compulsive viewing — from the comfort of a living-room armchair.

Key Issue

Bible Study notes

Implications

Prayer

Discuss this with others on the Connect Bible Studies website: www.connectbiblestudies.com

www.connectbiblestudies.com

linking the Word to the world

TV Game Shows

Part Three: The Weakest Link

There are no victims, only volunteers.
(Anne Robinson, *Annie Goes to Hollywood*, BBC)

Please read Using Connect Bible Studies *before leading a Bible study using this material.*

Opening Questions

Choose one of these questions.

Think of a time when you were humiliated. Describe your feelings.	Do you think Anne Robinson is being appallingly rude or just having fun?
Would you like to go on the show? Why?	Is testing knowledge worth rewarding?

Summary

The Weakest Link appeared almost unheeded on 14th August, 2000 as part of the BBC2 daytime schedules. It quickly gathered an avid following due to the radically new approach of the show's host, Anne Robinson who, rather than helping contestants to feel at ease, went out of her way to be rude and critical.

Fundamentally, this is a quiz show with a potential prize of £10,000. The contestants are asked general knowledge questions in rapid succession. At the end of every round, each contestant nominates the person they believe to be 'The Weakest Link' — the person who they feel contributed least to accumulating more prize money. Anne issues a scathing rebuke to the person with the most nominations who then leaves the game via the 'Walk of Shame'. This contestant then has the opportunity to comment on the team's performance and who they think will be voted off next time.

In the final round two contestants compete head-to-head for whatever prize money the team has accrued. With this end in mind, there is often strategic voting in the latter rounds as contestants try to ensure that their ultimate opponent will be one they can easily beat.

Key Issue: Mean TV

Anne Robinson on *The Weakest Link* has created quite a stir with her novel approach to hosting a quiz show. Not for her the encouraging compère! It seems that nerves of steel are required to survive her derogatory comments and the 'Walk of Shame'. So why is the programme successful? Do we enjoy watching other people being put down? Does it matter that politeness has been ditched? Do we care that the winner must consign everyone else to be 'The Weakest Link'? Can the Bible possibly have anything to say about this game show?

Bible Study

Choose one question from each section.

1.   'You are The Weakest Link. Goodbye' — Rudeness

I don't get a bonus for being nice. (Anne Robinson, *Annie Goes to Hollywood*, BBC)

 ♦   Read Proverbs 11:12; 12:18; 15:2; 22:11; 25:15; 25:23; 28:23. What are the consequences of how we speak to each other?

 ♦   Read James 3:1–18. Why is the tongue so dangerous? In verse 12, James asks a rhetorical question. What problem is he raising and how does he suggest we resolve it?

2.   The Walk of Shame — Humiliation

The Walk of Shame — it's humiliating, the fact that people know that you're appearing on the programme and you've done so badly. (Mac, contestant)

 ♦   Read Psalm 22. How does David's perspective on his situation progress through the psalm?

 ♦   Read 1 Corinthians 1:18–2:5. What is God's attitude to human wisdom and intelligence? How does Paul take courage in the face of humiliation?

3. Will the Votes Follow the Facts? — Unfairness

I think one of the most disappointing things is being voted off when you're the strongest person in the round. (Paul, contestant)

♦ Read Exodus 23:1–9. How would you sum up this passage? Are there any expressions of fairness here that you find surprising?

♦ Read Matthew 20:1–16. Why do the workers accuse the landowner of unfairness? How does he challenge their concept of what is fair? What should their attitude be?

4. Sudden Death — Defeat

I think Meg will probably be voted off in the next round. She's had one or two good rounds, she's had one or two bad rounds — it all depends on how the questions come. (Robyn, contestant)

♦ Read Proverbs 1:20–33. When — and why — is defeat inevitable? How might it be avoided in this context?

♦ Read 2 Corinthians 1:3–11. What is Paul's perspective on defeat and difficulty?

Implications

I think, whoever takes the money home, there's only one winner and that's Anne.
(Jeff, contestant)

Choose one or more of the following questions.

- How much do manners matter? Are there limits to politeness?

- What would you say to a friend who finds Anne Robinson's put-downs hilarious?

- Have you been mean to someone lately? Or have you someone to forgive?

- Why can some people laugh off defeat whereas others feel humiliated by it? How do you deal with humiliation?

- How do you respond if you think something is unfair? What if you think God has been unfair?

- Has the Bible passage on defeat challenged your attitudes? How?

Prayer

Spend some time praying through these issues.

Background Reading

You will find links to some background reading on the Connect Bible Studies website:
www.connectbiblestudies.com/uk/catalogue/0006/background.htm

Discuss

Discuss this study in the online discussion forums at www.connectbiblestudies.com/discuss

Members' Sheet 3: *The Weakest Link*

Summary

The Weakest Link appeared almost unheeded on 14th August, 2000 as part of the BBC2 daytime schedules. It quickly gathered an avid following due to the radically new approach of the show's host, Anne Robinson who, rather than helping contestants to feel at ease, went out of her way to be rude and critical.

Fundamentally, this is a quiz show with a potential prize of £10,000. The contestants are asked general knowledge questions in rapid succession. At the end of every round, each contestant nominates the person they believe to be 'The Weakest Link' — the person who they feel contributed least to accumulating more prize money. Anne issues a scathing rebuke to the person with the most nominations who then leaves the game via the 'Walk of Shame'. This contestant then has the opportunity to comment on the team's performance and who they think will be voted off next time.

In the final round two contestants compete head-to-head for whatever prize money the team has accrued. With this end in mind, there is often strategic voting in the latter rounds as contestants try to ensure that their ultimate opponent will be one they can easily beat.

Key Issue

Bible Study notes

Implications

Prayer

www.connectbiblestudies.com

connect

linking the Word to the world

TV Game Shows

Part Four: Big Brother

I wanted a challenge for me ...
I wanted something different, and I got it.
(Stuart, 36, housemate)

Please read Using Connect Bible Studies *before leading a Bible study using this material.*

Opening Questions

Choose one of these questions.

Do people know the real you?	Would you like to be famous? Why?
What would be the best and worst thing about being on Big Brother?	Out of all the contestants, who would you have liked to win Big Brother?

Summary

50,000 people applied to live in the *Big Brother* house for the second series in 2001. Whether it was the prospect of instant fame or the £70,000 prize, there was sufficient incentive to overcome any doubts about being watched by millions of people for nine weeks.

The ten contestants enter the house with one suitcase of belongings. Cameras watch their every move 24 hours a day and edited highlights are broadcast on Channel 4 every evening. Meanwhile, the digital channel, E4, has 20-hour-a-day coverage and the *Big Brother* website allows fans to watch constantly through a choice of several cameras. The contestants have two weeks to get to know one another before the evictions begin. *Big Brother* calls them into the Diary Room one by one to nominate two housemates each. They are not allowed to discuss their nominations with the others and must now account for their choices to *Big Brother*. Viewers participate in a phone vote to determine which of the two housemates with most nominations will leave the house at the end of the week gand, ultimately, who the winner will be.

Each week *Big Brother* sets the housemates a task that tests their ability to work as a team. This often reveals characteristics that individuals would prefer to keep hidden — an angry moment often leads to nomination and then eviction.

Key Issue: Being On TV

Big Brother was groundbreaking television as it replaced actors and scripts with 'ordinary people' and 'ordinary lives'. Instantly successful, this new style game show had hit upon a captivating formula. It mixed competition with the stuff of 'normal' life — relating, eating, drinking, learning, being. Suddenly the day-to-day interactions we all experience took on new implications as the participants vied with each other to win. 'Ordinary' people had their moments of fame as their every move was watched, and suddenly there was a new topic of gossip for the viewers. So what does the Bible say about fame, and behaviour in the limelight? Does it talk about the attraction of voyeurism, or the temptation to show off? What does it say to people who would like to be on television?

Bible Study

Choose one question from each section.

1. Being On Show

I am a poseur — I am a poseur! (Stuart, watching himself following eviction)

- ◆ Read Isaiah 58:1–12. What motivated the Israelites to fast? What was wrong with this and what was God looking for?

  See also Isaiah 29:13.

- ◆ Read Matthew 23:23–28. What did Jesus condemn in the Pharisees' behaviour and attitudes?

  See also Luke 20:45–47.

2. Being Known

From very early on I wanted to be a pop star ... When I go to the Big Brother House, I feel that it might be the extraordinary thing that I never actually did as a pop star — I think going in there would fill that sort of hole that's in my life at the moment. (Dean, 37, housemate)

- ◆ Read 2 Chronicles 26. How did Uzziah's fame go to his head? What lesson did God teach him?

- Read Matthew 23:1–12. What did the Pharisees love about their place in society? What did Jesus think of them?

  Note that the Pharisees were highly respected within Jewish society — they were the conservative religious establishment.

3. Being Watched

The ten new housemates have already been in the house for 35 hours … For the next 62 days their every move will be watched by 33 cameras. Witness now their final moments of freedom … (narrator)

- Read 2 Samuel 11:1–17. Trace David's path from a sleepless night to adultery and murder. How could he have avoided the sins?

- Read Matthew 5:27–30. What is the principle behind Jesus' radical words? How does 'just looking' become sinful?

4. Being Talked About

The people that really understand this is us. (Stuart, 36, housemate)

- Read Jeremiah 9:2–9. What is wrong with gossip? Why does Jeremiah link gossip with a refusal to acknowledge God?

- Read Matthew 12:33–37. How is gossip an aspect of what Jesus was talking about? What do our words reveal about us?

Implications

I did like me in the house — I am a nice guy, believe it or not. (Stuart, 36, housemate)

Choose one or more of the following questions.

- What would you say to someone who thinks God must be like *Big Brother* — critically watching your every move?

- What would you do if your friends started gossiping negatively about the people in *Big Brother* — or about anyone else?

- Are there things you see that tempt you to sin? What can you do about this?

- What are the dangers in being famous, even if that fame is relatively trivial?

- Do you like to be noticed for what you do? How can you receive your sense of worth and value from God instead?

- How wise is it to watch TV shows you have reservations about, in order to talk to your friends who like them?

Prayer

Spend some time praying through these issues.

Background Reading

You will find links to some background reading on the Connect Bible Studies website: www.connectbiblestudies.com/uk/catalogue/0006/background.htm

Discuss

Discuss this study in the online discussion forums at www.connectbiblestudies.com/discuss

Members' Sheet 4: *Big Brother*

Summary

50,000 people applied to live in the *Big Brother* house for the second series in 2001. Whether it was the prospect of instant fame or the £70,000 prize, there was sufficient incentive to overcome any doubts about being watched by millions of people for nine weeks.

The ten contestants enter the house with one suitcase of belongings. Cameras watch their every move 24 hours a day and edited highlights are broadcast on Channel 4 every evening. Meanwhile, the digital channel, E4, has 20-hour-a-day coverage and the *Big Brother* website allows fans to watch constantly through a choice of several cameras. The contestants have two weeks to get to know one another before the evictions begin. *Big Brother* calls them into the Diary Room one by one to nominate two housemates each. They are not allowed to discuss their nominations with the others and must now account for their choices to *Big Brother*. Viewers participate in a phone vote to determine which of the two housemates with most nominations will leave the house at the end of the week and, ultimately, who the winner will be.

Each week Big Brother sets the housemates a task that tests their ability to work as a team. This often reveals characteristics that individuals would prefer to keep hidden — an angry moment often leads to nomination and then eviction.

Key Issue

Bible Study notes

Implications

Prayer

Discuss this with others on the Connect Bible Studies website: www.connectbiblestudies.com